Montville Township Public Library
90 Horseneck Road
Montville, N.J. 07045-9626
973-402-0900

Library Hours

Monday	9 a.m.-9 p.m.
Tuesday	9 a.m.-9 p.m.
Wednesday	9 a.m.-9 p.m.
Thursday	9 a.m.-9 p.m.
Friday	9 a.m.-6 p.m.
Saturday	9 a.m.-5 p.m.
Sunday	12 p.m.-5 p.m.

see website www.montvillelibrary.org

★

FUN & CREATIVE
WORKSHOP ACTIVITIES

COOL
ENGINE & MOTOR
PROJECTS

REBECCA FELIX

**Checkerboard
Library**

An Imprint of Abdo Publishing
abdopublishing.com

ABDOPUBLISHING.COM

Published by Abdo Publishing, a division of ABDO, PO Box 398166, Minneapolis, Minnesota 55439. Copyright © 2017 by Abdo Consulting Group, Inc. International copyrights reserved in all countries. No part of this book may be reproduced in any form without written permission from the publisher. Checkerboard Library™ is a trademark and logo of Abdo Publishing.

Printed in the United States of America, North Mankato, Minnesota
062016
092016

Design and Production: Mighty Media, Inc.
Series Editor: Paige V. Polinsky
Photo Credits: Rebecca Felix, Paige V. Polinsky, Shutterstock

The following manufacturers/names appearing in this book are trademarks: Duracell®, Energizer®

Publisher's Cataloging in Publication Data

Names: Felix, Rebecca, author.
Title: Cool engine & motor projects : fun & creative workshop activities / Rebecca Felix.
Other titles: Cool engine and motor projects
Description: Minneapolis, MN : Abdo Publishing, [2017] | Series: Cool industrial arts | Includes index.
Identifiers: LCCN 2016907650 | ISBN 9781680781267 (lib. bdg.) | ISBN 9781680775464 (ebook)
Subjects: LCSH: Electric motors--Juvenile literature.
Classification: DDC 621.46--dc23
LC record available at http://lccn.loc.gov/2016907650

TO ADULT HELPERS

This is your chance to help children learn about industrial arts! They will also develop new skills, gain confidence, and make cool things. These activities are designed to teach children how to work with engines and motors. Readers may need more assistance for some activities than others. Be there to offer guidance when they need it. Encourage them to do as much as they can on their own. Be a cheerleader for their creativity!

Look at the beginning of each project for its difficulty rating (EASY, INTERMEDIATE, ADVANCED).

TABLE (OF) CONTENTS

WHAT

ARE ENGINES + MOTORS?

We use engines and motors every day. Have you ever stored food in the fridge or ridden in a car? Have you ever used a hair dryer or a printer? Then you've used an engine! Engines convert energy into motion. They are also called motors. The words *engine* and *motor* are both used to refer to devices that create motion. All engines need an energy source to create motion. This energy source can be water, air, fuel, heat, or electricity.

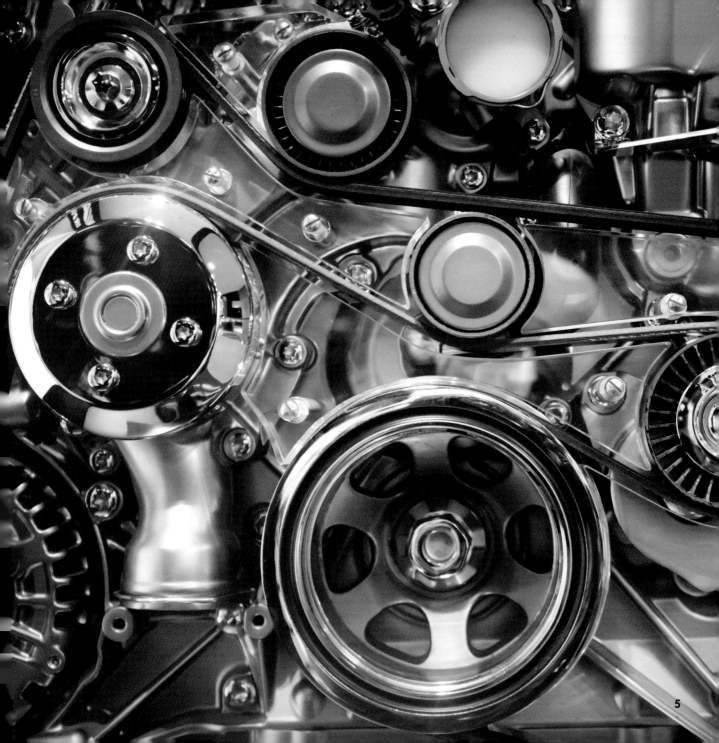

WORKING WITH ENGINES

Workshop Tips

It is important to set up a safe workspace when building motors. This workspace can be almost anywhere. It can be in the garage, in the basement, or at the kitchen table. Just make sure you get **permission**! Then, follow the tips below to work safely.

- Keep your workspace clean and free of clutter. A moving motor can catch loose objects, and the flame of a heat engine can start a fire if it's too near clutter!

- Get adult help when wiring, using knives, and lighting and controlling flames.

- Only set a motor in motion if you are there to watch it. Never leave it running while you look or walk away.

- Motors can get very hot. Handle project parts carefully even after the motor is shut off!

- Most importantly, *always be alert!*

Essential Safety Gear

- Gloves

- Safety goggles

- Face mask

- Closed-toe shoes

Be Prepared

- Read the entire project before you begin.

- Make sure you have everything you need to do the project.

- Follow the directions carefully.

- Clean up after you are finished.

ADULT HELPERS

Working with engines can be **dangerous**. They can **involve** using sharp tools, flames, and electricity. That means you should have an adult standing by for some of these projects.

KEY SYMBOLS

In this book, you may see one or more symbols at the beginning of a project. Here is what they mean:

SUPER SHARP!
A sharp tool is needed.
Get help!

HOT!
This project requires hot tools. Handle with caution.

FACE MASK
Doing this project creates dust or requires glues with strong odors. A face mask should be worn for protection.

TOOLS OF THE TRADE

Here are some of the materials you will need for the projects in this book.

3VDC MICRO VIBRATION MOTOR

3-VOLT WATCH BATTERY

ALUMINUM TUBING

D BATTERIES

ELECTRICAL TAPE

FLAT COPPER WIRE

FLORAL FOAM

FOAM TAPE

GALVANIZED WIRE

INSULATED
COPPER WIRE

INSULATED
SPEAKER WIRE

JAR CANDLE

PLIERS

SANDPAPER

SCRAP WOOD

STRONG MAGNETS

TEA LIGHT

TOILET PAPER TUBE

WIRE CUTTER

WIRE STRIPPER

SPINNING STARS CAMPFIRE

CREATE A HEAT ENGINE
THAT LOOKS LIKE A
CAMPFIRE AND SPINS
A STARRY SPIRAL!

MATERIALS

- pencil
- red, orange, yellow, & brown construction paper
- scissors
- tape
- tall jar candle
- blue acrylic paint
- paintbrush
- thin paper plate
- small star stickers
- large floral foam base
- wire cutter
- 16-gauge galvanized wire
- needle
- 6" (15 cm) thread
- lighter or match

DECORATING THE JAR

Draw flames on the red, orange, and yellow construction paper. Cut them out. Draw logs on the brown paper. Cut them out. Tape the flames and logs around the candle.

CREATING THE SPIRAL

Paint both sides of the paper plate blue. Let it dry.

2 Draw a **spiral** on the plate. Cut along the line. Stop cutting when you reach the center.

3 Decorate the spiral with star stickers. Set aside.

Continued on the next page.

11

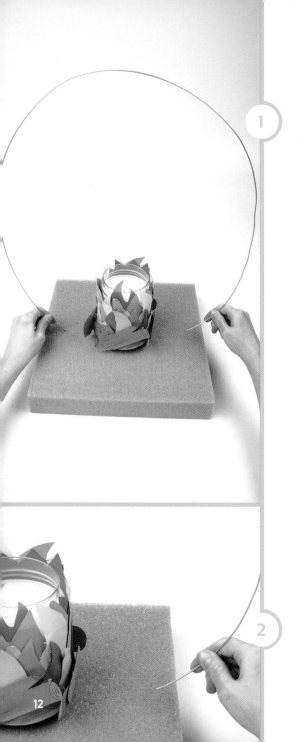

CREATING THE WIRE HANGER

1. Set the candle on the foam base. Cut a piece of wire about 3 feet (0.9 m) long. Bend it over the candle in an arch. Make sure the top of the wire is high above the candle.

2. Stick the ends of the wire into the foam base on each side of the candle.

FINISHING + LIGHTING

1. Thread the needle. Carefully poke it through the top of the star **spiral**.

2. Tie several knots in the thread on the underside of the spiral. Make sure the knot won't slip through when you hold the spiral up with the thread.

3 Bend the top of the wire arch down a bit. Drape the thread over the bend. Pull the thread until the **spiral** hangs above the candle. Make sure it doesn't touch the candle. Tie the thread to the wire. You can also trim the end of the spiral if it's still too long.

4 Light the candle. Make sure the spiral is *not* touching the flame. Soon, the heat should rise and make the spiral spin! If it doesn't, try adjusting the spiral's height.

FOAM
STEAM ENGINE
SHIP

SCULPT A SHIP AND
BOIL WATER IN A TUBE
TO MAKE IT MOVE!

SCULPTING THE SHIP

1 Set the foam brick on the cutting board. Use the knife to carve off two long corners, turning the bottom into a *U* shape.

2 Carve a thin rectangle out of the other side of the foam. Make sure the surface you carve is smooth and level. This is the back of the boat.

CUTTING THE TUBING

1 Cut a piece of tubing 22 inches (56 cm) long. Set the extra tubing aside.

Continued on the next page.

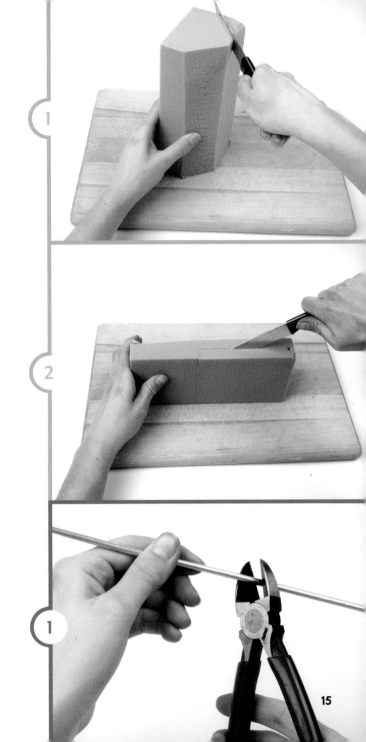

15

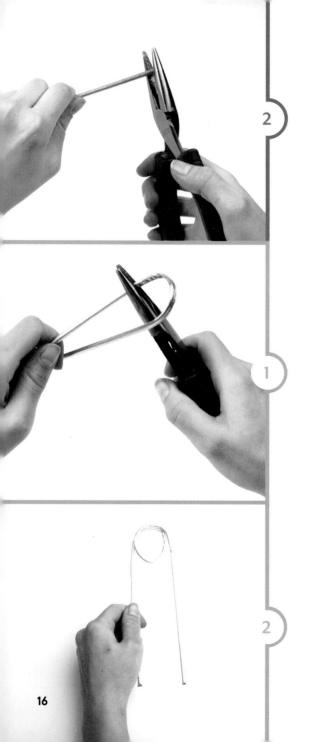

2 Use the pliers to pinch both ends of the tubing shut. This will keep debris out later when you push the tube through the foam.

BENDING THE TUBING

1 Measure about 7 inches (18 cm) from the end of the tube. Use the pliers to begin bending the tube. Move the pliers very slowly along the tube! If you bend one spot too much or too quickly, it can break or crack.

2 Bend the tube until you have made a coil about the size of the tea light.

3 About 1 inch (2.5 cm) from the coil, carefully bend each end of the tube up.

4 About 1 inch (2.5 cm) from the bend, carefully bend each end back the other way.

5 Hold the tubing so the coil is **horizontal**. The entire piece should resemble an upward stair-step.

Continued on the next page.

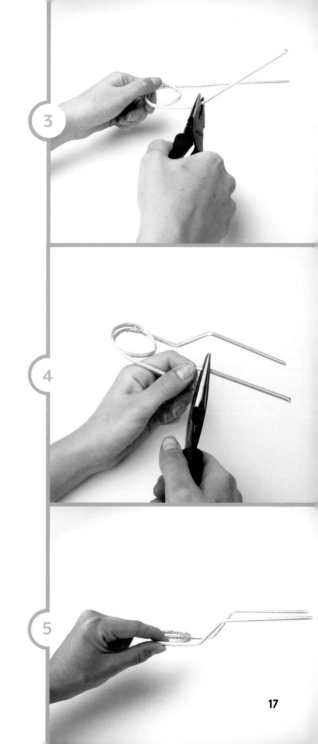

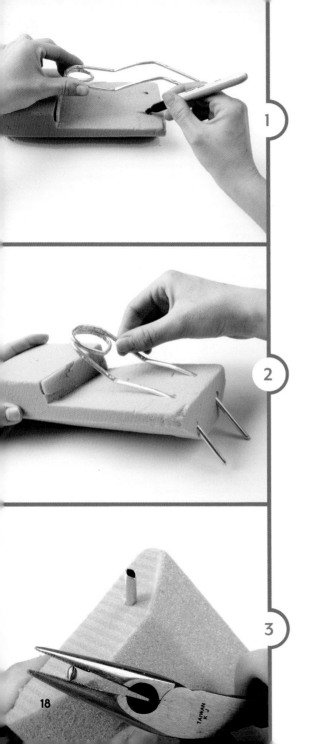

INSERTING + FILLING THE TUBING

1 Make two marks near the back edge of the boat. Space them as far apart as the ends of the tubing.

2 Push the ends of the tube into the marks at an angle. They should poke out the back of the boat.

3 Once the ends are through the foam, pinch them with the pliers to open them.

> ### TIP
> Make fun accessories out of craft foam and glue them to toothpicks! You can make a flag, buoy, and more!

4 Fill the tub with a few inches of water. Push the entire boat underwater and hold until bubbles come out of the tube ends. This fills the tube with water. This is a key step in making the engine work!

LIGHTING + MOVING

1 Keeping the tube ends under water, let the ship rise to the water's surface.

2 Place the tea light under the coil. Light the candle. Then wait and watch! The candle boils the water inside the tube. This creates steam. This steam pushes water out of the tubes, which moves the boat forward!

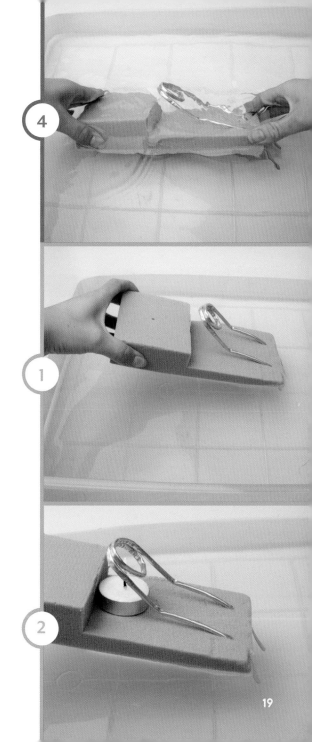

BUZZING ROBOT

USE A MINI MOTOR TO CREATE A ROBOT THAT BUZZES AND MOVES!

BUILDING THE BASE

1. Paint the cardboard and toilet paper tube. Let the paint dry.

2. Cut the cardboard into any shape you like. It will be the robot's base. Then cut two loops off the toilet paper roll. These will be the robot's body and head.

3. Cut the flat copper wire into four 1-inch (2.5 cm) pieces. Use the pliers to bend each piece into an S shape. These are the robot's legs.

4. Tape the legs to the bottom of the base.

Continued on the next page.

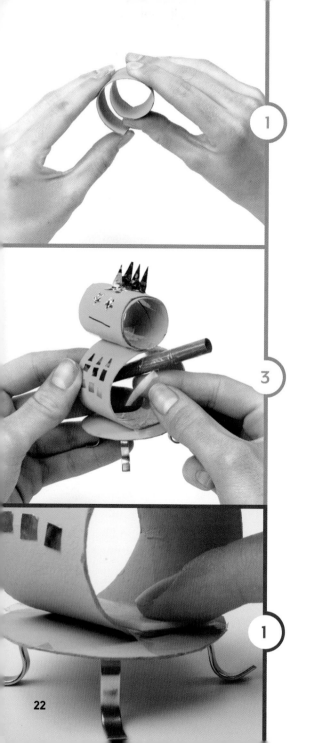

CREATING THE ROBOT

1   Cut one side of one of the toilet paper tube loops. Then roll the loop to make it smaller. Tape the edge to secure. This is the robot's head.

2   Tape the other loop to the base. It is the body. Decorate the body with markers or stickers. Tape on the head and decorate it too!

3   Roll a piece of construction paper into a tube. Make it a little longer than the body is wide. Tape it inside the robot body for the arms.

SETTING + WIRING THE MOTOR

1   Cut a piece of foam tape about 1 inch (2.5 cm) long. Place it inside the robot body, on top of the base.

2 Check that the ends of both motor wires are **stripped**. If they are not, use the wire stripper to remove a bit of **insulation** from each wire end.

3 Test the motor with the battery. Press one stripped wire end against each side of the battery. Did the motor buzz? If not, switch the wires to the opposite sides of the battery.

Continued on the next page.

23

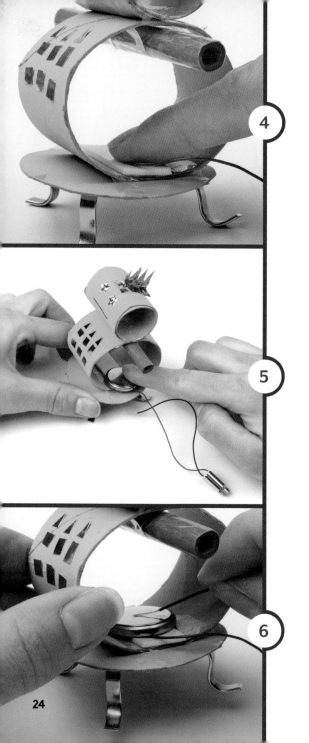

4 Press the end of one wire into the foam tape near one end.

5 Press the battery onto the wire.

6 Touch the other wire to the battery to make sure it works. Then remove the wire.

EVEN COOLER

Get creative and experiment! See how tall you can make your robot without the motor toppling it over. Then see if you can make a wider robot or one with more or fewer legs!

7 Press the motor onto the other end of the tape. Make sure its **rotor** is able to spin freely.

8 Place a small piece of electrical tape on the end of the loose motor wire. Tape the wire to the top of the battery. The motor should come to life! Watch your robot buzz across a flat surface! Untape the top wire to turn the motor off.

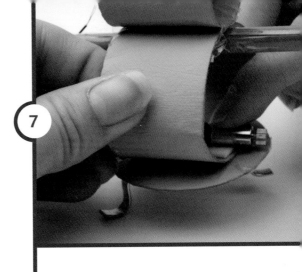

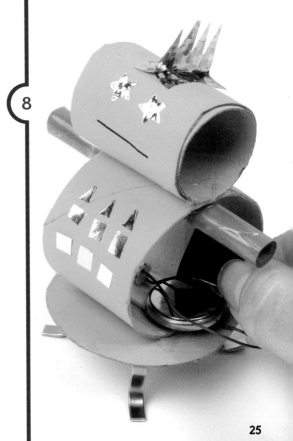

FLIPPING GYMNAST+
MYSTERY MOTOR

MAKE A MAGNETIC MOTOR AND WATCH A TINY GYMNAST SPIN AND FLIP!

MATERIALS

- 22-gauge insulated copper wire
- ruler
- scissors
- 100-grit sandpaper
- D battery
- electrical tape
- permanent marker
- paper
- colored markers
- pencil
- clear tape
- acrylic paint
- paintbrushes
- piece of scrap wood
- insulated speaker wire
- wire stripper
- foam tape
- 2 large paper clips
- 2 to 3 strong magnets

MAKING THE COIL

1 Cut 30 inches (76 cm) of the copper wire. Sand about 3 inches (7.6 cm) of each end.

2 Wrap the wire tightly around the battery. Leave a straight tail at both ends.

3 Slide the coil off the battery. Pinch it together in a circle. Wrap the ends around the coiled circle a few times on opposite sides.

Continued on the next page.

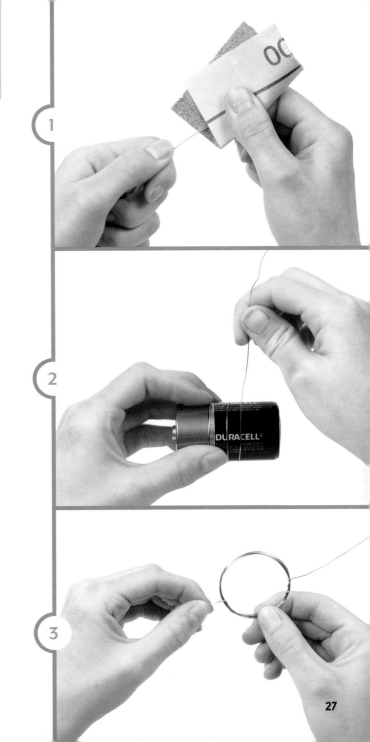

4 Use a very small piece of electrical tape to keep the coils wrapped tightly together. There should be no space between the loops.

5 Hold the coil with the ends pointing straight out to the sides. Carefully color only the top of each end with the permanent marker.

MAKING + ADDING THE GYMNAST

1 Fold the piece of paper in half. Along the fold, color a 2-inch (5 cm) square one color.

2 Draw the outline of a gymnast on the colored square. The fold should be at the bottom of the gymnast's feet.

3 Cut out the gymnast. It should be connected at the feet and a different color on each side.

4 Put the bottom of the coil in the fold between the gymnast's feet. Tape the gymnast's head to the top of the coil.

MAKING THE PLATFORM + FINISHING

1 Paint the scrap wood a fun color. Let it dry. This will be your base.

2 Cut two pieces of speaker wire. Make them each a little shorter than the base.

3 **Strip** 1 inch (2.5 cm) off both ends of both pieces of speaker wire.

4 Use electrical tape to attach one end of each wire to each of the battery's **terminals**.

Continued on the next page.

29

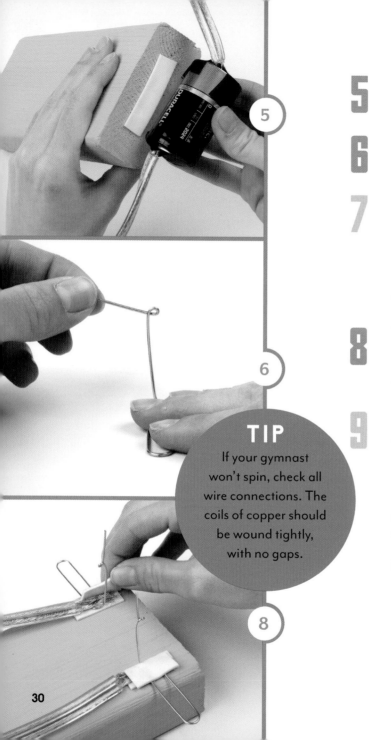

5 Attach the battery to one end of the base with foam tape.

6 Bend the long wire of each paper clip into a loop as shown.

7 Use foam tape to attach the paper clips across from each other on the wood base. Make sure the paper clip loops are the same height and facing each other.

8 Tape each loose end of the speaker wire over a paper clip with foam tape.

9 Place the ends of the coil in the paper clip loops. **Stack** the magnets and set them directly under the coil. The coil should start to sway! Give it a small spin. Watch the gymnast take over and spin at top speed!

TIP

If your gymnast won't spin, check all wire connections. The coils of copper should be wound tightly, with no gaps.

GLOSSARY

DANGEROUS – able or likely to cause harm or injury.

HORIZONTAL – going side to side, parallel to the ground.

INSULATION – material used to keep something from losing or transferring electricity, heat, or sound.

INVOLVE – to require certain parts or actions.

PERMISSION – when a person in charge says it is okay to do something.

ROTOR – a machine part that spins around another part.

SPIRAL – a pattern that winds in a circle.

STACK – to put things on top of each other.

STRIP – to remove a wire's insulating outer layer. A stripped wire has had its outer layer removed.

TERMINAL – a device attached to the end of something for the purpose of making an electrical connection.

Websites

To learn more about Cool Industrial Arts, visit **booklinks.abdopublishing.com**. These links are routinely monitored and updated to provide the most current information available.

INDEX